THERE IS NO DARKNESS

POEMS ON SHAKESPEAREAN QUOTES

DR. SONIA GUPTA

DEDICATED TO
MY DEAR FATHER

O' my dad was an English teacher,
He usually talked about quotes of Shakespeare,
Telling the meaning hidden in those lines,
He motivated me for the life time.

He often used to tell me casually,
O' why don't you write poems on this legendry?
I kept on telling, "Ok dad, I will do one day for you"
And he said, "But, foreword I will write for you".

Alas! destiny had some other plans,
He left me all alone within a glance,
He may be far away, but always near,
His enchanting quotes, I today also hear.

O' today I picked up my pen and paper,
And scribbled his wish in these chapters,
Quotes are of someone's else, but my dad's memories,
Look, dad I fulfilled your wish.

Somewhere in the twinkling stars above high,
You might be looking at your daughter with a smile,
And that smile of yours is the glittering diamond,
O' dad, your teachings always enchant.

Contents

Contents

Contents

Foreword

Poems reflecting vivid shades of life

Quotes have always been a motivational booster for everyone. They are like enlightening candles in the gloom of life. With their silent words, they ignite inner enthusiasm and motivate the readers to accept life's challenges and move on. The unique power harboured by these quotes is the deep meaning and message hidden within a few words. Poetry is one of the famous forms of English literature that is a canvas painted in poet's ink of vivid emotions, feelings, and imaginations. But if quotes get incorporated into these poetic verses, they add more beauty to the composition.

"There is no Darkness" by Dr. Sonia Gupta consists of poems composed by her on William Shakespeare's Quotes reflecting vivid shades of life. This is a unique style of poetry I have come across that has a beautiful mix-up of quotes and verses.

Perhaps there is any person who does not know the famous name "William Shakespeare", who is the soul of English literature. He contributed in vivid areas of English literature through his melodious verses. He used certain lines in his dramatic representations which are considered to be Quotes composed by him. These quotes not only inspire everyone but also reflect the reality of this life and world. Dr. Sonia has composed these poems using some of those quotes.

Dr. Sonia Gupta is a versatile genius and a wonderful combination of mind, heart, and art. A dentist by profession with a passion for poetry and painting is a rare combination. Her profession reflects in her poetry too. Like a surgeon, in her poetry too, she peels and heals.
She has a powerful pen that instantly knits her experience into a poetic ecstasy that mirrors her inner feelings and sensitivity. Through her imaginary ink, she has composed such verses in which the meaning and message of the quote can be well perceived by the readers.

"The odd phase in life seems to be a dome of darkness,
And you get surrounded by worries and stress,
The truth is that there is no darkness but ignorance,
If you lose something, there is always another chance".

(There is no darkness but ignorance)

"O' All the world is a stage and we all are the actors,
Playing a unique role in life's each sphere,
When our role is finished, the curtains fall,
And after a specific period, life's story stalls".

(All the world is a stage)

Some quotes composed by William Shakespeare reflect the facts of life in a funny and humorous way and Dr. Sonia has also painted a unique picture using such funny words in her poetry.

"Sometimes they say that they had visited heaven,

Where with the angles of the Lord they had fun,

Sometimes they talk about fairy tales,

In which vivid roles they play".

(Dreamers often lie)

"So strange is your style and your way,

You change hundred times within a day,

How surprised it is to look at you dear,

God has given you one face, and you make yourself another".

(God has given you one face, and you make yourself another)

Poems in this collection reflect vivid shades and aspects of life.

O' wounds of miseries pierce the heart,

Igniting a pain in body's each part,

A gloom of despair darkens the surroundings,

Life becomes bare, left with nothing.

(Grief makes one hour ten)

"O' for the miserable, hope is a boon,

An enlightening candle even in the gloom,

The miserable have no other medicine but only hope,

With this hope, they can climb any rope".

(The miserable have no other medicine but only hope)

"This life is the right moment to do something,
It is silly to wait for things,
Things do not happen themselves,
We can make them happen ourselves".

(The golden age is before us, not behind us)

"The happiest are those, who have got a merry heart,
They live life joyfully even after death departs,
With its magical wand, it plays amazing miracles,
For it even pebble is diamond and thorn a petal".

(A merry heart goes all the way)

Dr. Sonia's poems are penned with a worshiping frame of mind as hymns of life, a divine inspiration direct from her heart that touches the reader's soul. It is a 'must read' poetry book that will soothe every ruffled heart and the wailing mind of modern man. Dr. Sonia is already an acknowledged and published poetess in Hindi and English with her thirteen independent books out of which nine are in English and four are in Hindi. I congratulate her on her 10th English poetry book and look forward to her achieving greater heights in the realm of literature. Let us hold this book in our hands and cherish the melody of these verses.

- CHANDRA PRAKASH SHARMA
Poet, writer, reviewer
Patiala, Punjab, India.

Preface

"The lunatic, the lover, and the poet, are of imagination all compact."
William Shakespeare

Very well said by the renowned poet and dramatist *William Shakespeare,* through the above quote that the lunatic, the lover, and the poet are gifted with imagination but the poet has the power of the pen to ink his imagination. The poets can paint a beautiful canvas in the hearts of the readers which is worthwhile to preserve forever. They are capable of observing things internally that others may not.

Quotes are the most common booster of motivations. Since the beginning of our school time we are taught to learn these thoughts by our teachers and parents. English literature is very wonderful consisting of mixture of forms especially in poetry and prose that is really a unique.

William Shakespeare was a great legend and a well-known name in the field of English literature which is totally incomplete without him. His verses today also enchant a melody in vivid forms of poetry, whether any sonnet or drama. He has contributed in every area, whether tragedy, motivation, fun or romance. His every quote is unique and in little words, speaks a lot.

My father (late sh. Devinder kumar) was an English teacher. And he often used to teach me life's lessons through Shakespeare's quotes. When he became aware about her daughter's writing skill, he used to say with a smile "Do write poems on his quotes, dear, people will really get motivated and inspired" .

And I noded the head "Ok papa, I will". And he again used to smile "write,, write,, I shall write a foreword for you". Alas! destiny had some other plans and he left this materialistic world forever. Today his wish is going to be fulfilled. Though he is not here to write the foreword for me, but his blessings are hidden in the verses of this collection.

The current book in your hands "Poems from Shakespeare's Quotes" is a collection of 50 poems which are composed using quotes written by the great poet and dramatist *William Shakespeare*. And the major theme behind these quotes is inspiration. Though I have written 9 poetry books till today, but this book is unique and different. May be, the message hidden in the poems is that all of us already know, but by incorporating Shakespeare's lines into any poem itself adds a melody into it. While writing these verses, every word reminded me of that great name who is considered to be the soul of English literature; the great *William Shakespeare,* and my dad who let me know about this great personality.

I hope all of you will enjoy reading this book and get drowned in the memories of our legend and the melody of these verses will enchant a music around you that will inspire and motivate everyone.

Without saying much let me finish here with a hope that as usual, my contribution will be appreciated by everyone around.

Yours truly
    Dr. Sonia Gupta

Acknowledgements

One can forget anything in life, but should never forget to thank someone who has helped us in any way. *Gratitude* is a single word, but deep meaning it holds. I usually hear these words -If we say Thank you to someone, it means we are bowing our head in front of that Lord only.

First of all, I thank the Goddess of words *Maa Saraswati,*who gave me the strength to complete this work and gave shape to my simple words to paint a beautiful canvas that would be worthwhile to preserve forever in the hearts of readers.

In this world, everything changes, but one thing that never ever changes is *our parents.* Heartfelt thanks to my parents for their faith and showering their infinite blessings on me! Special thanks to my father who has left this materialistic world attaining the embrace of the divine Lord. He had been my inspiration and will be forever and his teachings illuminate my life's pathway like an enlightening candle.

A Token of thanks to *Chandra Parkash Sharma* sir, for reviewing and editing my book and writing a wonderful foreword. Without your guidance, this book could not be completed. Thank you sir for all your blessings and support.

Teachers are the selfless builders of our life, A word of thanks to all my respected teachers who always showed me the right path in my life and brimmed my heart with their blessings.

Lovable token of gratitude to my *brothers, sisters, and all family*members for their love and support always.

Friends are the precious ornaments gifted by God, who without any blood relation, make a bonding of forever relation. My regard and love to all my friends far and near.

Last but not least, it will be unfair if I forget to thank the *Notion Press publication* through which my book is going to be published. Thanks to entire team for the cooperation.

Thank you, readers, fellow poets, and friends for all your love and appreciation.

DR. SONIA GUPTA

Biography Of The Poetess

Dr. Sonia Guptais an Oral Pathologist (BDS, MDS) from, Chandigarh in India. Though, a doctor by profession, poetry is her passion. She has been writing since 2006. She is a trilingual poetess and writes in English, Hindi, and Punjabi languages. She has established herself as a renowned poetess after getting her twelve independent poetry books, out of which three are in Hindi and nine are in English. This is her 10th independent English poetry book.

Dr Sonia's compositions reflect vivid forms of literature like poetry, stories, essays, letters, songs and many more. She has won several awards in writing competitions organized by various groups on Facebook and other literary platforms. She had won a gold and silver medal in a poetic world cup contest held by Nigeria in Feb and May 2018 respectively. She has been awarded PRASANNA JENN MEMORIAL AWARD- 2018 by the Asian Literary Society. She got 5th rank in the International Essay writing competition on 'Skin complexion discrimination' organized by literary society, India in March 2018, one of her essays 'Our role & responsibilities towards nation were selected in a national essay writing competition and is a part of book 'Youth as nation builders; a collection of 41 essays published by lab academia. She has been awarded several awards in Hindi literature too. And her Hindi compositions are part of various anthologies, newspapers, and magazines.

Her English poems have been published in more than 50 common anthologies such as " DIVINE MADNESS", "BOUQUETS OF LOVE & VERSES", "CHRISTMAS", "HUMANITY & PEACE" by Ardus Publications ; "THE REEEST VERSES" and "NIBSTEARS CAVE ANTHOLOGY FOR PEACE" by Nibstear society; "ROSES & RHYMES" by Serene publication; 'FRAGRANCE OF ASIA', 'YOU AND ME', 'INFINITY', 'EAST MET WEST', 'PEACE LOVER', 'HEARTISTRY', 'QUEEN', 'RAINDROPS OF LOVE', 'TENUOUS BREATHS OF GIRLS' by VISHWBHARTI RESEARCH CENTER; 'HOPE REBORNE','MERI KAHANI' By Lab academia; 'WORLD BOOK OF POETS' by Sourav Sarkar; 'FRAGRANCE OF LOVE', LEAVES OF POETREE' by Writtenrock publication; 'WORLD HEALING WORLD PEACE' by Inner child press; 'BUTTERFLY LOVE', 'GIGLING PEN', 'POETIC CHRISTMAS', I AM A WOMAN', 'THE GOLDEN CROP', 'SUMMER RAIN', 'HEAT IS ON', 'THE MILLINEAL POETS', 'ONLY YOU' by poetry planet; 'VASUDHA-2' by raindrop publication; 'COMPLEXION BASED DISCRIMINITIES' by Notion press; 'GLOMAG -18' by Cyberwit publication; 'STONE AEROPLANE', 'REPUBLIC DAY', 'BONJOUR FEVRIER', 'BUTTERFLY' 'CYNDRELLA' by Spectrum publication; 'CHRISTMAS', 'In the memory of 1952' by Poetry of moon; 'PETALS OF LOVE', 'GEMS OF POESY', 'KALEIDOSCOPE OF ASIA', 'UNTAMED THRILLS & SHRILLS' by Asian literary society; 'SPRING- WINDOW TO PEACE' by Poetry for peace group, 'WORLD POETRY ON LET THERE BE PEACE' by Global feternity of poets publication; 'GATHERING WORDS' by Lanere lekan; 'VOICE OF VOICELESS' by Yes 2 publication and many more.

She is aregular contributor to monthly online magazines like "Hall of poets", "Reflection" and "Glomag" and international journals like "Research Inspiration", "Research imbibition" & "Jai Maa Saraswati Gyandayani". Her poetic journey continues with a great endeavor. Her poetry and writings reflect her closeness and deep love for nature, life, and spirituality. For her, poetry is a God-gifted boon and she wishes to fly high wearing the wings of poetry. Her many projects are coming soon.

Besides poetry, she is fond of paintings, singing, cooking, knitting, designing, stitching and embroidery too. She has won many awards in art competitions too. Many of her paintings have been placed on the cover pages of various anthologies. She has even designed the cover page on her own for her two English anthologies. She has got her own blog, YouTube channel, Facebook page, and Instagram profile.

Dr. Sonia Gupta is also contributing to the literature of her own professional field. Her several scientific papers have been published in indexed national and international journals with the first authorship. She is also working as a reviewer of various journals. She has also written two textbooks on her subject of specialization in dentistry, which is under publication process. Presently, she is working as a faculty in a prestigious dental institute near her city. And along with her profession, she is enjoying her passion too.

CONTACT DETAILS

ADDRESS- #95/3, Adarsh Nagar, Dera Bassi, Dist: Mohali, Punjab-140507, India.

MOBILE- 6280420736, 8054951990

FACEBOOK ID - 100004964983747@facebook.com

FACEBOOK PAGE - https://www.facebook.com/sonia4840/

BLOG - http://drsoniablogspot.blogspot.in/

E MAIL - Sonia.4840@gmail.com

YOUTUBE CHANNEL https://www.youtube.com/channel/UCKF2jM5P8VDjZ9fBZLBTRHA

INSTAGRAM ID-https://instagram.com/gdrsonia?igshid=YmMyMTA2M2Y=

THERE IS NO
DARKNESS

(Poems On Shakespearean Quotes)

DR. SONIA GUPTA

1. "There is no darkness but ignorance."

O' why do you keep crumbling on things that you lack,
Why do you always get stuck in the pains looking back,
In the search of perfections, you lose much more,
You forget that this life is to love and adore.

The odd phase in life seems to be a dome of darkness,
And you get surrounded by worries and stress,
The truth is that there is no darkness but ignorance,
If you lose something, there is always another chance.

Look, the sun rises after crossing the gloom of night,
Bringing new morning, so energetic and bright,
Beautiful pictures are developed in the dark room,
Amidst murky pond, a lotus always blooms.

Same way is life; beyond darkness exists a heaven,
Eradicate the fear of hopelessness and tensions,
Open up your vision and see beyond darkness,
You will cherish all around shimmer of brightness.

Every dark pathway has a door to brightness,
You often ignore the way toward success,
Live life fully accepting all its failures,
See how you will cherish amazing miracles.

2. "All the world is a stage"

O' All the world is a stage and we all are the actors,
Playing a unique role in life's each sphere,
When our role is finished, the curtains fall,
And after a specific period, life's story stalls!

Sometimes portrayed as a joker, bringing smiles to others,
Wearing a face mask hiding own tears,
As a child, wearing the nostalgic divine hood,
Roaming as a hero and heroine in our youth!

Bound in vivid relations we love and care,
Sometimes burning in agony and anger,
Nobody knows when the story turns its pages,
We remain unaware of life's mysterious phases.

We are nothing, but puppets in divine's hands,
He only assigns a role, he only plans,
Performing good role, our story gets big applaud,
And even after death, we are remembered by the world.

Life is like a cinema with vivid shades and hues,
But the story of life is so very true,
Play your role in such a way,
That your name gets scribbled in people's heart one day.

3. "A merry heart goes all the way"

O' deep inside this body, there exists a heaven,
'Heart', a place more beautiful even than a garden,
It is a priceless jewel, God gifted boon,
Where the first seed of any feeling is sown.

The happiest are those, who have got a merry heart,
They live life joyfully even after death departs,
With its magical wand, it plays amazing miracles,
A merry heart goes all the way even amidst hurdles.

It smiles like a flower even in odds and downs,
It crosses hurdles happily, winning successful crowns,
It sings melodious songs even in mournful moments,
It can even make others' life blessed and pleasant.

O' for it, even the desert appears to be a garden,
Even in the scorching summer, it enjoys drizzling rain,
It loves even withered rusty leaves of autumn,
In the bare life, it can fill colors of passion.

A merry heart can touch millions of souls around,
It spreads smile and love miles of smiles abound,
O' dear do not run after beauty and complexion,
Behold a merry heart; you will cherish life as heaven.

4. "Dreamers often lie"

O' look, dreamers are so amazing,
Wearing the wings of fantasy they cherish so many things,
They say they could see the sky in the earth,
They narrate so many stories of their last birth.

Holding stars, sun, and moon in hands,
Bringing magic with some magical wand,
All around they can see the bed of roses,
In their dreams, they touch the golden trees.

Sometimes they say that they had visited heaven,
Where with the angles of the Lord they had fun,
Sometimes they talk about fairy tales,
In which vivid roles they play.

Sometime they dance like butterfly on blooming petals in garden,
Becoming a fish and shark they float in blue ocean,
Sometime they meet their soulmate whispering love words,
They get drowned in its sweet nectar drinking the cup of love.

O' what a wonderful imagination they have,
Making everything so unbelievable in fact,
Do not you feel funny about the way they describe,
It's said very true that dreamers often lie.

5. "False face must hide what the false heart don't know."

O' it is very easy to wear a fake face mask,
It is very easy to pretend false,
So many emotions, so many eternal feelings,
Hidden behind our artificial smiling.

Sometimes the heart is pierced and the soul is torn,
On life's pathway we are left all alone,
But we assume to be brave and careless,
Who knows the real facts.

Sometimes life seems to be unfair,
We float in the ocean of despair,
Yet, we keep a fake smile on our face,
And move on in life's race.

Sometimes, there is none with us,
Yet, we pretend that whole world is with us,
In reality, we are surrounded by gloom,
But like the blooming flower we bloom.

True love, tender pains, and inner scars,
Can't be hidden so easily behind the fake mask,
It needs courage to artificially show,
False face to hide what the false heart don't know.

6. "Small cheer and great welcome make a merry feast."

O' there is a great joy in doing little things,
Greeting, motivating, and appreciating,
It doesn't cost anything to bring smiles to others,
Keep on smiling even hiding your own tears.

It is the moment in hands that matters,
Who knows what is written in the book of future,
Without any grudges, enjoy the present,
Make your surroundings lovable and pleasant.

Even the small poses captured in cameras,
Paint a kaleidoscopic canvas,
Threading a garland of vivid memories,
That is a boon amidst life's miseries.

Little smile and warm gesture,
Can enrich someone's life like an elixir,
Soothing balm for their unhealed pains,
Opening all the suffocating chains.

With your generous heart treat other people,
You will see how you can bring miracles,
It isn't essential to stage a big occasion to greet,
Sometimes small cheer and great welcome make a merry feast.

7. "No legacy is so rich as honesty."

O' we are gifted with so many jewels,
But honesty is one of the precious pearls,
A virtue that provides a feeling of peace,
Purifies one's heart and soul, free from guilts.

In today's time though difficult to speak the truth,
But honesty enriches us with profound mirth,
No fear of any excuses and manipulations,
Wisely leads to accomplishing all ambitions.

It is as pure as the ripples of flowing water,
As innocent as a little child's laughter,
Away from this world's myths and agony,
Honesty creates a temple of harmony.

In the era of corruptions and betrayal
It needs courage to indulge truth as ideal
But it maintains one's self dignity
Enlightening a candle of serenity.

O' no legacy is so rich as honesty,
It is considered to be the best policy,
Let us all get ornamented by this boon,
We will cherish this world as heaven soon.

8. "Cowards die many times before their deaths; the valiant never taste of death but once."

O' people usually ask what do winners do differently?
Why are they unique and appreciated by everyone?
It is simple, they do not do anything different in reality,
But they act in different ways for their mission.

Winners are the valiants that never lose determination,
They hold the weapons of courage and self-belief,
Even being failed, they try again and again,
They can do anything and achieve.

Winners are the warriors who fight till the end,
Without worrying about results,
Cowards only know how to defend,
Without putting any effort.

For winners, there is no day or night,
They don't stop until they achieve their aim,
They visualize their future so bright,
For them life is not an easy game.

Cowards are those, who mourn in death,
Embracing their fear, they lose their essence,
Cowards die many times before their death,
The valiant never taste of death but once.

9. "When we are born, we cry that we come to this great stage of fools."

O' when in the mother's womb we take breath,
We can feel the outside world before our birth,
Our tiny eyes become witnesses of this myth world,
Humanity is lost and all-around violence and hatred fuelled.

Our well-wishers become the worst enemies one day,
Every relation is just mean and fake,
Some keep smiling wearing a fake mask,
There is a light but still, all around there is dark.

Nobody cares for anyone here,
Even being everything around life is left bare,
People here play a game of faux pas,
They keep on worrying about others' tasks.

Human is ready to harm other human,
Holding in hands guns and weapons,
Little children scream becoming victim of those crimes,
Innocent faces cry with mournful rhymes.

Our face smiles looking at the humans,
He is merely a puppet in God's hands,
Alas! He considers himself the king of the pool,
When we are born, we cry that we come to this great stage of fools.

10. "Do not waste your love on someone, who does not value it."

O' love is not just a word, but heart to heart connection,
Away from boundaries of any cast or religion,
It is a garland threaded with pearls of faith and trust,
It is a divine feeling, not just lust.

Love is a blessing that showers joy and prosperity,
To value each other and give priority,
Hiding own tears bringing smiles to others,
Nourishing with nutrients of selfless affection and care.

Love is a feeling that can't be expressed in words,
It needs a pure heart to express,
It is not a show-off act,
It is an emotion that dwells in the heart.

Love is to dwell peace and harmony,
Love is to spread divine serenity,
Love is a priceless treasure of life,
It can make us win any strife.

Love is to respect and understand mutually,
It is to forget the little mistakes looking silly,
Love someone who cares for your feelings and means it,
Do not waste your love on someone, who does not value it.

11. "It is not in the stars to hold our destiny but in ourselves."

O' we keep on cursing the stars for our misfortune,
We keep on complaining that our life is just a dome,
But the fact is that our own Karmas matter,
It is not in the stars to hold our destiny but in ourselves.

This life is ours, depends on us how do we live,
Whether we cross challenges or simply leave,
Which path do we follow and tread ?
What are our virtues and what are our deeds?

It depends on us which thoughts do we knit,
What kind of future do we build,
Whether we want to move on,
Or over past just to crumble on.

O' it is simple, what we sow, so shall we reap,
There is value of every single deed,
Rather than cursing stars, we must concentrate on ourselves,
Remember this life is our test to act the best.

Take care of your every deed you perform,

With good deeds your life can be transformed,
Destiny is nothing but fruit of our deeds,
Stars can't hold your destiny indeed.

12. "There is nothing either good or bad, but thinking makes it so."

O' our mind is the master controller of our life,
It entwines vivid thoughts inside,
These thoughts give birth to our thinking,
That becomes the base of our living.

It is all the game of thoughts what we think,
One can seek goodness even in the sins,
For one, even the cruel seems to be most beautiful,
For others, even a diamond is just coal.

Someone loves even the prickly thorns and mud,
For someone, even wasteless are the blooming petals and buds,
For someone, even the gloom looks so bright,
For someone, there is gloom even in the light.

But the fact is that we all are God's creations,
Nobody is perfect in the real sense,
There is nothing either good or bad, but thinking makes it so,
It all depends on what seeds our mind sows.

Nourish your mind with divine thoughts,
You will cherish a beauty even in odds,
Thoughts can either make or break,
Their mystery is amazing, not fake.

13. "How far that little candle throws his beams! So shines a good deed in a weary world"

O' this world is a murky ocean,
Enclosed by the gloom of despair,
Sometimes it seems to be barren,
Everything looks so unpleasant and unfair.
But your single good deed can change everything,
Making this murky world a paradise,
You can eradicate so many sufferings,
Bringing all-around a smile.

With your single pious act,
You can change the world,
There is a different way and tact,
That you can spread all around love.

A good deed has a magical power though 'little' it seems,
None can even imagine what impacts it has dwelled,
How far that little candle throws his beams,
So shines a good deed in a weary world.

So, sow seeds of good seeds

And see the wonderful magic,
Performing good deeds,
You can cherish joy majestic.

14. "In time we hate that which we often fear."

O' being humans we are afraid of many things,
Many challenges and struggles we keep on facing,
But as we grow up in the life,
We begin to learn how to survive.

And a moment comes when we achieve our aim,
We realize that all our fear was just in vain,
Fear is a worm that engulfs our self-potential,
Turning even the possible into impossible.

Fear is a poison that kills us silently,
Dwells all around despair and agony,
It is vulnerable to being stuck in fear,
We forget all joy and cheer.

Fear is our worst enemy,
That takes away all peace and harmony,
Pushing us toward the door of hell,
It makes us weak and incapable.

It looks so silly to crumble over failures,
We yearn to achieve more adventures,
Aha! those struggles, accomplishments later we cheer,
And in time we hate that which we often fear.

15. "We know what we are, but know not what we may be."

O' everyone of us is blessed with so much potential,
That we can turn even impossible into possible,
We do have power and energy within,
But we forget this fact often.

We can carve diamonds from coals,
We can achieve any toughest goals,
We can enlighten a candle even in the dark,
We can leave a spell with our magical spark.

Alas! the fact is that we ignore everything,
And just keep on mourning,
We have a golden opportunity, but we waste it,
We know what we are, but know not what we may be.

Have faith in yourself and broaden your vision,
You can accomplish even more than you imagine,
The only thing needed is to know your potential,
You can cherish amazing miracles.

Once you illuminate this flicker of self-belief,
Anything in the life you can achieve,
Then you will smile at yourself,
O' what injustice we were doing for ourselves.

16. "With mirth and laughter let old wrinkles come."

O' life is too short, why keep on mourning,
There is a bundle of joy hidden in little things,
Live every moment joyfully burying all worries,
Forget about all pains and miseries.

Enlighten a candle of smile in your heart,
You will cherish profound mirth till death departs,
Dance freely to the rhythm of this life,
Sing a melody without any device.

Why to worry drowned in your sorrows?
Who knows what is written in the book of tomorrow,
All we have is present in our hands,
Cherish every moment without missing any chance.

Moments gather together become memories forever,
Thread a garland with pearls of mirth and laughter,
Even if you get old, have joy and fun,
With mirth and laughter let old wrinkles come.

Skin may be wrinkled, body may get weak,
But your innocent smile always greets,

Like a blooming lotus even in the pond,
Like a smiling rose even with thorns.

17. "God has given you one face, and you make yourself another."

What has happened to you O, man?
Why you pretend to be something else every moment?
Why do you keep an artificial smile?
And within you keep on burning like a missile.

O' you pretend to be a well-wisher from outside,
And sow the seeds of envy inside,
Showing empathy and compassion for others,
And from within you curse yourself.

One side you talk about love,
But deep within you dwell hatred,
On one side, you talk about bravery,
And deep inside you always worry.

One side you clap at other's success,
And deep inside you sow seed of stress,
One side you talk about ambitions,
And deep inside you lack determination.

So strange is your style and your way,
You change hundred times within a day,
How surprised it is to look at you dear,
God has given you one face, and you make yourself another.

18. "Grief makes one-hour ten."

O' wounds of miseries pierce the heart,
Igniting a pain in body's each part,
A gloom of despair darkens the surroundings,
Life becomes bare, left with nothing.

Eyes get flooded with tears and the soul gets torn,
When amidst suffering we are left all alone,
Nobody is there to share our pain,
Life seems to be unfair and in vain.

We sail in the sail of hopelessness,
And forget the word 'happiness',
No desire is left to live anymore,
When grief opens the miserable door.

We start cursing ourselves,
Why we have got this birth?
Millions of thoughts embrace our mind,
We start doubting even on divine.

O' moment of grief is very pathetic,
It engulfs all joy being so toxic,
Truly said, grief takes away all fun
Ah! this grief makes one hour ten.

19. "Better three hours too soon than a minute too late."

O' time is the master controller of life,
It can turn anything to any side,
Learn to respect its value always,
Avoid being indiscipline and late.

Every single second is crucial,
If utilized, it can bring miracles,
If wasted, you can lose opportunities,
Time is not a slave of anybody.

Like the sand in the hands, it slips away,
Wearing its wings it flies without delay,
Like a flowing river, it never ceases its flow,
Not visible, not held, can't be caged like a crow.

Have you ever looked at mother nature?
Every task of her is accomplished in time here,
Even death knocks at life's door at its fixed turn,
Before that, it can't embrace anyone.
The whole world revolves around its embrace,

Time is a weapon that can either destroys or make,
Why be late and let others wait?
Better three hours too soon than a minute too late.

20. "To do a great right do a little wrong."

O' we all remain afraid of the word 'wrong',
We regret thinking about what will happen,
But the truth is that mistakes are the best teachers,
That teaches us life's real chapters.

Have you heard of great legendries?
How did they all attain glory?
Failing several times and doing wrong,
They achieved the identity to which today they belong.

The mistakes reshape our potential,
We can do something new and special,
They open new gateways for us,
And guide us to perceive more success.

Don't worry if you do something wrong,
To do a great right do a little wrong,
Do little wrong and achieve great right,
By few mistakes, make the future bright.

The mistakes show us the right mirror,
Teaching us to fight with our fear,
Making us strong and capable,
They introduce us with our self-potential.

21. "The empty vessel makes the loudest sound."

O' who says that only words can shout?
Sometimes, silence speaks a loud,
Sometimes, we are broken from the inside,
Dwelling an emptiness and void.

Our heart is empty, yet full of pain,
Pierced by wounds that our own have given,
We wish to cry but can't cry a loud,
We keep mourning surrounded by dark clouds.

Heart dwells in bareness and agony,
Full of suffocation and melancholy,
We sail in the boat despair,
None is left near and, dear.

We yearn to embrace some shoulder,
But fail to find any well-wisher,
Everything around is dull and empty,
We don't wish to live actually.

The world thinks that we are all right,
But they can't see the other side,
Sometimes, nothing is fair all around,
The empty vessel makes the loudest sound.

22. "All is well when ends well."

O' life is too short to live,
Learn to forget and forgive,
We love ourselves for the silly mistakes,
Then why do we hate others if a little they fake.

We are humans and it is well known,
That 'to err is human',
Then why carry on things?
Why keep on complaining?

Let us forget them and move on,
Nothing is in your hands O' man,
The only thing you can do is to ignore,
And new avenues you should explore.

Keep aside all grudges and envy,
Let there be peace and empathy,
Inside your heart don't let hatred dwell,
All is well when ends well.

Life is precious, we get it only once,
Why waste in taking revenge,
Live every moment joyfully,
You will find this life beautiful actually.

23. We came into the world like brother and brother; And now let's go hand in hand, not one before another.

O' we all are same God's creation,
We all are God's children,
Living under the same sky and on the same earth,
He only gave us this human birth.

Like tiny alphabets united to form pages,
A building is formed with union of bricks,
Like rivers united to flow into ocean,
We all are one, we all are humans.

Alas! what has happened to us today?
Why everyone has got their own way?
We have dwelled so much hatred inside,
Why do so many differences reside?

Let us erase all differences and cheer,
Let us all get united, O' dear,

We came into the world like brother and brother,
And now let's go hand in hand, not one before another.

Let us enjoy the boon of unity,
And let us see the beauty in diversity,
Let us just dwell on humanity,
We all are humans, live with peace and tranquillity.

24. Knowledge is the wing wherewith we fly to heaven.

O' knowledge is the treasure that we earn,
It makes us wise and differences spurns,
It teaches us life's lessons,
It is a silent weapon with which any war can be won.

It enlightens a candle of wisdom within,
It keeps us away from all envies and sins,
Teaches to distinguish between right and wrong,
Knowledge makes us capable and strong.

It can turn a poor into rich,
It brings miracles with its magical stick,
Learn the power of this single word,
One can conquer the entire world.

O' knowledge is a light amidst murk,
Illuminating life with its spark,
It can lead toward the way of success,
Making us aware about real facts.

It is said that little knowledge is a dangerous thing,
Without knowledge life is nothing,
Always make the knowledge your companion,
Knowledge is the wing wherewith we can fly to heaven.

25. "Words are easy, like the wind; Faithful friends are hard to find."

O' we all are blessed with so many gifts,
Friends are one of the precious boons, so sweet,
Faithful bonding between two unknown hearts,
Away from agony, envy, and hatred.

Like blooming flowers in the fertile garden of life,
Special friends bring all the way a smile,
Like a candle of hope in the gloom of hopelessness,
A song of peace in worries and stress.

They accept us even with our imperfections,
Helping hands even in unfavourable situations,
O' they have got some miraculous power indeed,
Without saying anything everything they can read.

With wonderful colors of friendship they paint a canvas,
Bringing eternal joy and ecstasy till death departs,
O' they splendid sunshine and moonlight,
Most precious treasure of our life.

A bonding that provides life to dormant emotions,
A key to open success becoming motivation,
Friendship is the most pious relation and so divine,
Words are easy, like the wind; Faithful friends are hard to find.

26. "Pleasure and action make the hours seem short."

O' what an awesome feeling,
Joyfully doing something,
With a smile putting efforts toward our ambitions,
Without any worry moving toward our destination.

A little pleasure can turn into biggest happiness,
Millions of hearts can be touched by a little joyful act,
Everyone wishes to live those moments again,
We forget all our worries and pains.

Selflessly giving joy to others,
Brings a smile and peace for us,
Joyfully helping any helpless,
Takes away all our stress.

Pleasure is the rarest treasure,
That brims heart with laughter,
Things done in the embrace of pleasure,
Scribble life's unbelievable chapters.

Everything runs so smoothly,
When we do things joyfully,
It seems as if we have hit a big shot,
Pleasure and action make the hours seem short.

27. "The eyes are the window to your soul."

O' you are blessed with two beautiful eyes,
Through which you can admire everything outside,
The eyes are the windows to your soul,
They see what your soul beholds.

Open these windows and dwell love within,
Don't allow these windows to witness crimes and sin,
Let there be empathy and compassion,
Paint them with the colors of passion.
lit a lamp of peace here,
Looking at these let everyone smile and cheer,
Let these windows open doors of prosperity,
Bringing peace and harmony.

Let these eyes admire the beauty around,
Let these smile with smiles abound,
Let these eyes capture divine power,
Let these eyes witness humanity forever

O' these are not just windows,
But a special place where miracles are stored,
You can cherish the whole world as a paradise,
Your eyes reflect what is inside.

28. "To weep is to make less the depth of grief."

O' keep your grief alive within,
It is not worth crying and worrying,
Pain is a scar that reminds us of the wound,
It alerts us with a silent sound.
It is easy to shed tears,
But with tears actually your heart shear,
Flowing all moments that you faced,
Moving on to life's pathway and race.
Your grief is your biggest strength,
That acts as a silent weapon,
Killing your weakness within,
Makes you perfect in decision making.

O' weeping is not the solution,
You can't avoid the situation,
Grief provides more potential to self-belief,
To weep is to make less the depth of grief.

Rather keep this flame igniting within,

Learn from the pain it brings,
You will see, you will get up again,
And will realize that crying over was in vain.

29. "The miserable have no other medicine, but only hope."

O' hope is a four-letter word,
Yet around it revolves the whole world,
It is a fuel that keeps us alive,
Otherwise, who knows when we may die.

Sometimes, life seems to be so unfair,
We get drowned in the ocean of despair,
Nobody is there with whom we can share,
Everything seems to be empty and bare.

Yet, there is a flicker that keeps on illuminating,
With its glitter, it keeps on shimmering,
Giving courage that everything will be fine,
Don't worry about anything, leave it on time.

O' look, roses bloom along with thorns,
Lotus blooms in murky pond,
Illuminating this flicker of hope,
With every odd they can cope.

O' for the miserable, hope is a boon,
An enlightening candle even in gloom,
The miserable have no other medicine but only hope,
With this hope, they can climb any rope.

30. "When sorrows come, they come not single spies, but in battalions."

O' sometimes, darkened clouds surround us,
Making our life a fuss,
We try to solve one problem,
And another has already come.

We get drowned in the ocean of despair,
We find life to be totally unfair,
Broken we are from inside,
We don't wish to live this life.

We sail in the sail of hopelessness,
And another obstacle brings stress,
It looks as if a mansion is made,
In which a dreadful soul stays.

O' agony dwells in the heart,
Shearing our every part,
We fail to accept the truth,
That we are in the embrace of dearth.

Then we are left all alone,
And feel this truth said by someone,
When sorrows come, they come not single spies, but in battalions,
Yes, it was well said by someone.

31. "The golden age is before us, not behind us."

O' we keep on waiting for the right time to come,
And we waste whatever life welcomes,
The life we get is rare, we get only once,
We must achieve high goals and aims.

This life is the right moment to do something,
It is silly to wait for things,
Things do not happen themselves,
We can make them happen ourselves.

Self-determination and zeal for doing something,
Can lead to achieve great things,
We can scribble a golden story,
We can attain memorable glory.

Moment in hands is the most crucial,
Who know what is written in future,
Who knows what is beyond ages,
Who knows the story of new page

O' we consider this life to be short,
We avoid putting any effort,
And we forget one fact in all this mess,
The golden age is before us, not behind us.

32. "Out, out, brief candle! Lives but a walking shadow."

O' life is like a candle,
Candle casts the shadows,
Maybe large or little,
But it never loses its glow.

O' one shadow produces another shadow,
And the light keeps on illuminating,
The same way this life beholds,
Even after death, a new beginning.

Look, life of a candle is too short,
Until the period of night to come,
In the same way, life is too short,
Until the call of the death comes.

Look, candle burns with its flame,
But for a short time,
Same way life sometimes plays a dreadful game,
But again sings a melodious rhyme.

O' but both never die,

One image vanishes,
Another produced besides,
After one life, there is another life.

33. "Every offence is not a hate at first."

O' offence is not just from the beginning,
It takes birth from certain happenings,
Sometimes, we love someone at the very first sight,
We wish to take a long flight.

The whole world seems to be a paradise,
In our life, that person resides,
We trust in him blindly,
And considers him our everything.

Alas! with time moving on we realize,
That the person was a misguide,
Who betrayed us in such a way,
That we get broken since that day.

And that love turns into offence,
We start doubting our essence,
We fear to trust anyone more,
We close our heart's door.

Then we can perceive this fact,
Every offence is not hating first,
It is the product of certain things,
Which led to the development of offence.

34. "What's done can't be undone."

O' it is silly to cry over the past,
For the things that happened while doing our tasks,
You can't change what has happened,
What's done can't be undone.

Instead of crying and repenting,
Learn from those happenings,
Move ahead with a new lesson,
That you will not repeat them.

O' the steps you take, are very crucial,
They can lead you to either heaven or hell,
Take these steps very cautiously on life's track,
Once you take, you can't turn back.

Forget if by mistake you did wrong,
Ignore, learn and move on,
It is true that you can't change the past,
But you can take care of the upcoming tasks.

Life is not always unfair,

Another chance is always there,
Welcome every opportunity with open arms,
You will cherish life's real charms.

35. "Some rise by sin and some by virtue fall."

O' this world is very strange,
Destiny here plays sometimes a game,
Sometimes people put so many efforts,
Even then they don't achieve deserving results.

Alas! sometimes it is totally unexpected,
Lie gets awarded and truth is rejected,
Undeserving people attain everything,
And capable lose each and everything.

There are faces which wear a face mask,
Yet, they are revived in every task,
Some are blessed with innocence,
Yet, they have to bear penitence.

Some embrace always a garland of flowers,
Some have to walk on thorns however,
Though everyone is known to be human,
Yet there is a vast of difference.

Some get everything doing nothing,
Some lack everything despite doing everything,
Some rise by sin and some by virtue fall,
O' look, what happens around the world, it is so small.

36. "Nothing can come of nothing."

O' it needs a courage to do something,
If you don't put any effort, you can't achieve anything,
You have to take steps with determination,
That can lead you to accomplish your mission.

Even God does not help those who don't help themselves,
He becomes a guide to those who wish to guide themselves,
He will not always be the saviour,
He also leaves when efforts are put off by others.

O' to have something, first, you have to nourish yourself,
For getting the crop, you have to sow the seed first,
Even the cultivated land turns to be barren,
If it perceives no nutrients.
Listen to those glorious stories,
How they attained glories,
Sacrificing so much and putting efforts,
Then they achieved the shining results.

If a well is empty, no water it can provide,
If eyes are empty, none can cry,
O' it is the universal truth for everything,
Nothing can come of nothing.

37. "In the end truth will out."

O' millions of lie you can speak,
But this word 'lie' is so very weak,
Today it seems to be friendly,
Tomorrow it will prove to be enemy.

O' you can wear a face mask,
But you can't hide your heart,
Whatever truth it beholds,
That is forever, crystal gold.

O' truth is bitter, but the best friend,
That keeps you burden-free till the end,
No need to hide anything from anyone,
You can speak boldly to everyone.

Lie is like the bird flying in the sky,
For a moment it touches the heights so high,
But if its wings are broken,
Very miserably from the height it is fallen.

O' telling lies you may shout,

But, in the end, the truth will out,
Truth has the power to demask lies,
The lie is like a bird, that will fly.

38. "One fire burns out another 's burning, one pain is lessened by another's anguish."

O' time has changed a lot today,
No love, no humanity, left in life's pathway,
Human is hurting another human for their own self,
Deep inside envy and hatred have dwelled.

No compassion, no kindness, no empathy,
All around blowing a breeze of cruelty,
Holding guns and bullets in their hands,
Making so many cruel plans.

People don't have equal rights to live,
They can't do what they wish,
Everyone has chosen their own way,
Creating something unexpected every day.

Nobody cares about other's grief,
Rather, giving others pain, another feel relief,
Alas! Human has become so mean and selfish,

One fire burns out another 's burning and one pain is lessened by
another's anguish.

O' God, look at your creation,
Do we call them human?
In front of your divine eyes,
World is following a wrong side.

39. "A fool thinks himself to be wise, but a wise man knows himself to be a fool."

O' this world is so strange, different people it beholds,
Some are like coal, some are like gold,
The ones who are wise, consider themselves novice,
And fool always thinks he has a brilliant choice.

Fool has little knowledge and experience,
Yet he considers himself to be the most genius,
Wise is the ocean of knowledge, yet wants to learn more,
His ways are simple, and he never leaves to explore.

A fool considers himself the king of kings,
Who Flies wearing the egoistic wings,
While wise seems to be down to earth,
His heart is enriched with profound mirth.

A fool thinks that he can conquer entire universe,
For wise, yet lot has to be accomplished,
For fool, every power is in hands,
Wise follows meaningful plans.

O' what a mystery, what a difference,
Even though both are humans,
A fool always remains anguish and wise supercool,
A fool thinks himself to be wise, but a wise man knows himself to be a
fool.

40. "Be great in act, as you have been in thought."

O' our thoughts give us an identity,
They reflect our essence and reality,
Alas! sometimes we play a duel role,
Act differently from the thoughts we behold.

We must follow and respect our every thought,
We should only express what the mind beholds,
As our thoughts are pure and generous,
We must do things with heartiness.

O' it is of no use to have ideal thoughts,
And performing deeds that are at odds,
It is worthless to think wise,
And in reality to act another side.

O' dear, there is no need to wear a face mask,
With honesty, you must accomplish every task,
Behold the heart and mind of crystal gold,
Be great in act, as you have been in thought.

Do whatever, there is in your heart,
Don't say something and perform any other task,
Thoughts are your own reflection,
Do not let them to be in vain.

41. "Love all, trust a few, do wrong to none."

O' this life is a boon we get it once,
Why waste on grudges and arrogance?
Yes, it is your life, you have to decide,
Without bothering about what is others' choice.

O' everyone has got their own style,
Own way of perceiving this life,
Don't disregard anyone's opinion,
With a true heart, listen to everyone.

O' be generous and compassionate,
Learn to love and not to hate,
Admire their ways of loving,
Don't expect in return anything.

With your heartiness appreciate others,
Read their life's written chapters,
Learn from their golden words,
Listen to whatever they whisper.

Very wisely treat others,
Don't disregard their gestures,
With a lovable smile, greet everyone,
Love all, trust a few, do wrong to none.

42. "Suspicion always haunts the guilty mind."

O' doubt is our biggest enemy,
Engulfing all peace and harmony,
Sowing a seed of suspicion in mind,
It can snatch everything which we call 'it's mine',

It is a silent killer that kills every relation,
Even it kills our self-confidence,
In its embrace, even right seems to be wrong,
Everything is hell if suspicion is along.

O' it will leave you only in a guilt,
No relations you can build,
It will create an ocean of solitude,
Taking away all your dudes.

O' keep away this word 'suspicion',
Never ever make it your companion,
It is a virtue that is arrogant and unkind,
Suspicion always haunts the guilty mind.
Throw away this devil from within,

It will force you to commit sins,
Burying all humanity of yours,
It will only build an inhuman nature.

43. "Fair is foul, and foul is fair."

O' this life is strange, and strange is this world,
Strange things around it beholds,
Fair is foul, and foul is fair,
Everyone wears a fake mask here.

Love; an awesome feeling, but a sweet poison,
Vey cleverly betrays and pierces the heart of someone,
Glamour and glory; so fascinating to achieve,
Unfolding, reveal cruelty that you can't perceive.

Look, destiny seems to be unfair and unacceptable many times,
But crossing gloomy pathways we cherish bright sunshine,
Ah! so difficult it is to face failures and frowns,
But in the veil of failure there are hidden successful crowns.

O' rose looks so pretty, but stays within thorns,
Murky is that pond, but beautiful lotus here blooms,
Desert looks so amazing, yet burns under scorching sun,
Pearl is so precious, yet resides with creatures of ocean!

Amazing is that artist, wonderful is his creation,
Sometimes heaven is actually hell and the hell is heaven,
Nobody can judge which is real?
This world is so strange, harbouring everything duel.

44. "If we are true to ourselves, we cannot be false to anyone."

O' be true to yourself, whatever may be the situation,
Your inner conscience is your reflection,
Never ever try to cheat yourself, even in your solace,
Your inner soul is a pious divine place.

Being true to ourselves is like cherishing peace,
No guilt remains within, nothing else to seek,
You confess everything to your inner self,
Then no matter, what will be the result.

A true person knows the real side of lie,
It will lead to repentance and we mournfully cry,
At that time, nobody is there to console,
And we get broken as a whole.

A true person can feel the emotions of someone,
He knows that lie is like a prickly thorn,
If we are true to ourselves, we can't be false to anyone,
If we have faith in ourselves, then only we can be faithful to someone.

Being true to ourselves is the most beautiful virtue,

You can't perform any bad deeds if you are true,
First thing is to be true for yourself,
Then only you can feel proud of yourself.

45. "Expectation is the root of all heartache."

O' we all have expectations being human beings,
Love, care, affection and many things,
Having faith and trust on others,
We Keep expectations more than ourselves.

O' dear, leave expectation from others,
It will bring only pain and tears,
From within if it is not fulfilled,
It put us under a burden of guilt.

Dwelling in agony and melancholy,
Expectation hurts us deeply,
Creating all-around a gloom of despair,
Life seems to be totally unfair.

O' expectations lead to violence,
Hatred, ego, and arrogance,
Burn like an igniting fire within,
If not accomplished, lead to sin.

If you wish to live life peacefully,
Stop expecting from others completely,
Expectations never give, but always take,
The expectation is the root of all heartache.

46. "Thoughts are but dreams till their effects are tried."

O' all of us think that we will do this and that,
We weave our dreams and go on that track,
Thoughts are the builders of our ambitions,
They set our goals and missions.

But to turn our dreams into reality,
We have to put effort fully,
We can't achieve the results, unless we act on,
We start doubting the thoughts that we dwell on.

O' thoughts weave dreams and dreams are our guide,
Thoughts are but dreams till their effects are tried,
Dare to turn dreams into truth,
Give your sincere efforts and input.

Without hard work, we can't achieve nothing,
It is better to stop dreaming,
If you don't believe in yourself,
There is no use to build a dreamland for self.

It is not that dreams don't come true,
Dreams one day become real for you,
It depends on totally you,
Whether you wish them to be true.

47. "Have more than you show, speak less than you know."

O' dear, live this life being wise,
Don't disclose everything that is inside,
This world is a play stage,
Everyone here is so strange.

People will judge you every time,
You can't impress them every time,
Keep yourself into a boundary,
No need to tell everything to everybody.

O' take every step cautiously,
Don't trust anyone blindly,
You can't satisfy everyone,
Even if you disclose your plans.

Keep the ocean of knowledge flowing,
Don't speak anything without knowing,
Never think that you are fully perfect,
Remember this life is a test.

Be humble and intelligent,
Don't be egoistic and arrogant,
Have more than you show,
Speak less than you know.

48. "Always the wrong person gives you the right lesson in life."

O' this world is very strange,
People play here an unexpected game,
Sometimes you meet someone,
Who hurts you without any weapon.

Someone pierce your heart in such a way,
That you don't wish to live anyway,
But by getting betrayed you get awakened,
And you realize what they had actually done.

Sometimes even your own beloveds betray,
Leaving you all alone and astray,
And you are totally broken,
Can't trust again on someone.

Sometimes you follow someone blindly,
Without knowing his reality,
And behind your presence,
He digs a well for which you repent.

Grief is there, but it also encloses happiness,
Teaching you this world's secrets,
And you learn to know how to survive,
Always the wrong person gives you the right lesson in life.

49. "Speak what we feel, not what we ought to say."

O' dear, we must be true to ourselves,
There is no need to cheat ourselves,
Say whatever you think is right,
Nothing to fear, nothing to hide.

O' you are the leader of your life,
How you live is your choice,
Listen to your heart what it says,
And follow your own ways.

O' if you find anything wrong, dare to speak,
Don't consider yourself a coward or weak,
And if your heart doesn't allow for anything,
Don't just nod your head for everything.

O' don't be duplicate in anything,
What your heart speaks, say that thing,
Remember everything you should honestly say,
Speak what we feel, not what we ought to say.

In this fake and duplicate world,
People hold a strange sword,
Dare to cut the power of that weapon,
Speak, whatever you wish to speak O' man.

50. "Make not your thoughts your prisons"

O' deep inside your body,
There is a wonderful factory,
That entwines tiny threads,
To knit a complicated cobweb,

O' magical are these thoughts,
Either provoke or evoke,
Like the strings of the chariot,
They try to keep you in your control.

It is up to you, O' human being,
How do you control these strings,
Never let these thoughts go astray,
Never allow them to follow the wrong way.

Make not your thoughts your prisons,
Make them an epitome of wisdom,
Create every thought cautiously,
Master your mind to think soulfully.

Life is all about mindset,
Which thoughts it possesses,
Nourish them with positive nutrients,
You will cherish fruitful moments.

THERE IS NO
DARKNESS

(Poems On Shakespearean Quotes)

DR. SONIA GUPTA